Catching the Moment

Catching the Moment...

a take on
a lifetime

Some of these ParaShots have appeared in
Stand, Agenda, The Journal and other periodicals.

Gerry Wells

Matador
9 Priory Business Park,
Wistow Road, Kibworth Beauchamp,
Leicestershire. LE8 0RX
Tel: 0116 279 2299
Email: books@troubador.co.uk
Web: www.troubador.co.uk/matador
Twitter: @matadorbooks

ISBN 978 1789014 266

British Library Cataloguing in Publication Data.
A catalogue record for this book is available from the British Library.

Printed and bound by CPI Group (UK) Ltd, Croydon, CR0 4YY
Typeset in 12pt Times New Roman by Troubador Publishing Ltd, Leicester, UK

Matador is an imprint of Troubador Publishing Ltd

MIX
Paper from
responsible sources
FSC
www.fsc.org
FSC® C013604

For my family and friends with love.

(Best taken gently with a glass of something delicious…)

Contents

FRENCH CONNECTIONS

HOPE COVE

En Passant

Where I'm standing is sea bed at high water: another world
swims past - round fish, flat fish, and once a confused Mako
shark seriously off course - it checks out Newhaven harbour
causing a stir - columns in the local *Gazette*, beach warnings.
Popping tactile pustules off the overhanging bladder wrack,
I watch small yellow crab watching me from its crystal pool
left by the tide, wonder how I'd rate against a passing shark.

Early

You need a special star for this - a mile of beach, carapace
of upturned dinghy, coiled rope. Shackled by the iron chill
of a tide just on full, I watch another Turner sky complete,
and far out Royal Sovereign repeats its measured warning:
fog…fog…fog: inshore its spooks diminish in an early sun;
ankle grip of slack tide lasts just three minutes six seconds:
go back! I say - and it obeys. Canute might appreciate that.

God Shot

Sea and sand in three quarters, far Corsican pines in the fourth:
you can be god out here as well as playing the Vikings my blood
suggests; I had a friend who saw god as an Oxo cube, something
in the perfection of its shape he said: I couldn't see it, but sensed
insight which fired an *almost seen.* Then after being Viking for a
while I go back to Oxo cube for rethink on this sea-bed-to-desert
stage, my shadow lengthening, tide line wiping out my footprints.

Edging It

Lowest water inches deep, the sand's striations powering full stride
nearest I get to natural flight in my own driven space… a circle like
eternity, I running round it; the fog reduces to a shimmer of mirage
that never comes close, yields to the sharps and angles of that WW2
wreck beached with its treasure cargo of single malts' spill of glory:
story goes there wasn't a tern left unstoned along this coast – locals
either. In its shadow I skirt the raw tang of history feeling excluded.

Running the Radius

Force ten off Beachy Head, you slow-count the breaker
from crest to colonnade…*six seconds* – tight: two more
wolf grey, plumed, can't get better than *six…chicken* is
coming on starting at knees - count two more… *next or
never*… it's *go-go-go* into nightmare endless and arctic,
a pebble shrapnel over colonnade…you make it… just;
jelly-legged you wonder *why?* A riddle when you're ten.

Rite of Passage

A new moon has stolen the sea leaving sweet-scented pines,
Corsican, tight ranked against what fates will bring; I turn
seaward a mile out - moon power the lock on tide and time,
the errant tide rediscovered by feel - a staging for epiphany
mood driven in the privacy of emptiness with senses trigger
tight; sea's alive and rippling now - time lapsed… poised to
follow the pull of old imperatives: time to start for landfall.

Essential Beachcombing

More a mood thing… best after September storms,
tide not long ebbing; you need warm but no gloves,
they'll get wet, pockets fine. Not a beach day which
gives it an edge, a shingled mile with you sets stage,
possibilities rule Ok*:* that bottle with its last chance
message yet to come; today an ammonite fragment,
tiny conch shell pink, beautiful - a serendipity first.

Beachy Head

All that's implied by *the length of England* finishes here…a country
worth of everything from Carlisle to the ewe struck amazed enough
to stop chewing. Unusually it's windless now - and under my spread
weight, England drops five hundred feet sheer, though my eye notes
a hint of overhang - enough to offer a mind-blowing descent to those
requiring achievement…while others *en passant* who exhausted that
use an easier route to lighthouse level where ends/beginnings attend.

Beacon Build – 1936

Our space a perfect place - cliff-high, sea in/out
always there. Fire-builders tolerant: *fetch wood,
keep out from under...* they stash a cask of pitch
as foundation; we carry lovely driftwood magic,
burns hot orange, violets - it's a mountain when
it's done. Fired-up with history, our pitch bomb
paints its Goyas and we eye-to-eyeball Armadas.

An Open Beach

I learned this early… *it's unwise to piss into the wind,* ditto
when screaming. A flight of gulls is stacked up screaming
close in shore; wiser now, I turn down wind, add my voice
a litany mourning an empty beach where a full world once
lived - *The Huts,* a fleet drawn up, shelters of old tarpaulin
based on beach and belief - the women strong as their men,
children brown as nuts…desert now where salt winds play.

Once

The sea's adazzle: dragon loads of sapphire, the forever scent of sea - a memory scene stuck fast. But the *now* snaps back in facsimile exact as *then* putting on a show: *plus ca change* slips off to France a horizon away. I start to jog - lengthen into full flight, this lift-off sense that arrives once and never again, past old familiars, rock after eras of tide, straggles of seawrack, the breath of two worlds in congruence - on no other day than this.

Imperfections

It took time to sort this one - you thought the sea to be discreet, swallowing-up…then things became *au naturel*, and now it's in your face - a dog, dead, not stinky yet, stretched as if in deepest post-radial kip, home fire burning: your first taste… if you had a stick you'd poke it - then another world leaks in, an otherness you haven't felt before, something understood. You stare out to sea, its glittering gem stones staring back…*come on in* it smiles.

New Boy – 1939

On the quad steps we've reached the point of no return:
Dad hands over the pound note that has to last all term;
a wet kiss, firm handshake - then they've gone, finally to
dwindle into toll bridge and beyond. I take painful stock:
grey stone Gothic, the massive chapel intent on business;
it's a rite of passage we just do it Dad said. I wonder what
a *rite* is… then realise the end game - *you're on your own.*

Christmas 1940

Alfriston: *Ye Olde Star Inn* our stable; outside a sentry guards the Officers' Mess - it's Christmas card snowy, cold…not good for short-straw door-stepping. Phoney war's done, Dunkirk victory etc; seasonal fare's great, we stuff ourselves - hear out Harry's apocryphal tales in the bar. Christmas night comes explosion that's not old Santa C - it's RAF not making it back from Berlin.

Litlington Revisited

Still a Sussex boy with home flints underfoot:
crash site long past, sheep-grazed to the bone,
the only choice in desperate moments close to
the smallest Downland church, maybe a folly,
twenty souls' worth - room enough for a crew
to stand down in this heartland rung by larks
with blue Sussex sweep of sky their memorial.

Normans' Bay

With Sussex blood on a particular evening, you
might hear the flap of emptying sails, sounding
of keels into shingle: resonances, the din of men
in ominous no-haste readying for war, dressing
for conquest. Time rings down to the slack tide,
an after-the-lord-mayor's-show ennui - off duty
guard skimming boredom at imagined Harolds.

Dieppe... The Expendables 1941

Tanks parked from Meads to martyrdom, war score
circa 5 nil...general staff fidgety, bored troops worse
before departure; the salty breeze whispers *Dieppe...*
a now quiet town waiting, including Dieppe; the pubs
retrench - residents contemplating what tanks can do
without trying. A limbo of days sentimental at times:
then *The Plan* blows, a trial run for D day it was said.

(*Meads – Eastbourne's posh end*)

Back to School 1942

Paddington: no glass, gross barrage balloons overhead; *Sir Galahad* fizzing and steaming waits with Tom; early, we bag window seats as *All clear* sounds. Trains are dodgy… long stops in remote places, no heating, kit-bagged soldiery at station stops…all this at snail's pace. We change trains in blackout Hereford, notable for its three pickled eggs, eyeballs in a jar. In Ludlow it snows: no taxies. Matron makes cocoa no sugar as we doze on our feet…finally to bed. Mine's damp.

Home Guard Duty Ludlow 1943

A Shropshire evening-into-night… a languid Teme
with moonlight on its back bridged by water pipes:
serious enemy target we are told, *it supplies Ludlow.*
Bullshit. However daft the armies do it; I take first
stag; another first: I have live ammo…steel, tactile,
polished, the gun symbol and portent; now it's end
game, the river's voices taking it to its own destiny.

On The Lake – Moor Park 1943

I'm live centre, peace-cushioned by still waters running dark;
evening's busy: two owls in different registers, a vixen staking
out her patch, a mosquito's *zing*...safe place here with ancient
pike keeping an eye on things below; two sunsets this p.m. one
west the other east - Birmingham in blitzed mode too far away
to hear, agony reflecting off a cloudy sky. I think of lemmings,
the need for multiple death and what set the human narrative.

Tiger Moth View 1943

Towards dusk comes a clear sky - in my open cockpit it's cold
getting colder as we climb west for hazed Marches I know are
there; dipping our wings we trace a slow arc north...then east
to Wolverhampton stoking up its own artificial anti Luftwaffe
fog with its unforgettable smell. Odd parameters these... safe
Marches, a city under threat: actuality and *whyness* of it plays
on a beautiful stage; landing, we edge fog. Sometimes it works.

Further Education – 1943

You're seventeen with little time, your ferret searching
below; lie quiet, smell forest earth - noting that shadow
moving isn't tree…that twigs without cause don't snap:
understand your inheritance. New darkness fills space,
your hunter: he doesn't *know* but *senses* you. So, ferret
is down, breathe shallow, stay still, this darkness paints
in many shades: so it's eye-on-ball with such little time.

Prom Patrol - 1943

Obverse of the remembered… shut, shuttered - Wish Tower
to Pier midnight stint; moon path on sea poses spider-legged
pier, mid section removed; shingle to tide line's frazzled with
wire, impedimenta rooted in minefield; echoes of *we'll gather
lilac* long gone from blue bandstand; we clump heavy-booted
past where the deckchairs are not: it's obverse again: hot sun,
head-knotted hankies, sandals with socks - and mother asleep.

(*Wish Tower – coastal defence dating from Napoleonic times.*)

Merlins

A from-out-of-nowhere entrance opening doors:
Casablanca *here's looking at you kid* a grown up
time floating adolescence - that tongue-tied first
date leaving you sleepless, Benny Goodman, big
bands and a world changing with you... then the
low-fly crackle of strike attack - Spitfire flies off
into legend, those open doors closing one by one.

Enlisting – 1943

Starting early - Clee Hill afloat on private sea,
train to Hereford: recruiting sergeant's sharp,
shiny, waxy moustache you could spike dough
nuts on. Medical: starkers in icy cell - trapped
by testicle (amazed he found them) I'm told to
cough; so to IQ test, swap soul for the shilling,
then off for our rite of passage beer. Men now.

Call to Arms 1943

North begins at Watford – well past that now, blackout
dark is king - I watch it pass the window, see its shades,
like silence it seems incomplete... I reckon any *absolute*
lies in the head. I'm a number now - eight digits' worth
in transit now morphing to *expendable item soldiers for
the use of...* is this rebirth, is there life after? At 0500 I
become my number *get an effing haircut* someone says.

First Footing – Fire Order

The singular moment - how long it takes to reach
a process crafted to fit exactly what it has to find:
nerve ends transmitting to channels of perception
that will become the time-scored recurring worry,
this directive demanding all, denying even breath,
past, future - only a super focused *now* is relevant
to a vital step, a rebirth maybe. The step is taken.

First footing – Target

You're a dead man, you don't know it, shaving… blade's blunt, water's icy - saving what's hot for a brew: we do that, it's called *pride* I'm told; my gun sight's spot on exact - one touch…you're away with the fairies and I'm spare. Can you hear a Chanticleer somewhere behind you? Pissed off with Pertelote now it's dawn, he's got other things to see to… you haven't. Dry your face, how about teeth? Chanticleer chimes again. My heart bleeds a little.

Late Call

Memory striking… places which existed - others that scarcely did: Jurques, St. Pierre, the Bocage mapped by panzerfaust and hedge, Rouen… it seemed that redemption could come only by way of the sword: the laceration of soldier, community caught in wrong place at the wrong time. I was young, ignorant, swamped by fatigue and stink of cordite… but with understanding of why it was my Father had little to say of his time at Cambrai in 1917… Another journey.

ENSA up Front - February 1945

Set the scene and let her sing…

Cellar damp, brass monkey cold, air fogged in
with the unwashed, plus Capstan full strength;
in borrowed greatcoat she sings…Piaf perhaps
but subtle, guitarist a gentle escort to her voice
in a slow burn of lamplight; close to casual, she
brings back another world somewhere mislaid,
caressing now in sounds and otherness of song.

(ENSA – Entertainments National Service Association (1939/45)

Spring Attitudes – March 1945

The way in looks like overgrown rat hole - so duck first:
brick steps down to cellar, dry, dark as the ace of graves
without liberated oil lamps – home for now. Frau Hitler
bottled cherries for us: big, black full of all the summers
there ever were, sealed with expectations we all cling to -
trust as well when someone mentions poison: *put it on the
list* says Joe adding *haute cuisine* compo condensed to his.

Eggs

The enemy at his gates, he moves towards them;
old fields these, their tillage generations deep, he
their ransom; history like a tide on its turn, stills,
hags of the moment play with their dice and wait
for something to play for… the judgment of odds
stark on the baize of their game… *faites vos jeux!*
from the gun's length offering everything he has.

Men of Peace

Life by lantern... Matt far in foreign land is home,
nothing changes: the mare is dying, inside her foal
is alive... the German watching as Matt his enemy
kneels, investigates: foal's not a breech: so, the old
narrative again - slip knot, blind securing...timing
pull to mare's weak straining - finally foal. Then to
straw-drying life...old man in tears - men together.

Ending... Beginning

The German beckons...Matt, bloody to elbows follows
into kitchen; wife, maybe daughter, sits at a bare table
staring...*wasser, heiss* he snaps...*schnell!* Elbows deep
in the first hot water for weeks, Matt slow-soaking the
mare's blood - but he still stinks, is ashamed; breaking
silence the old man's *danke* speaks for more than a life.
Outside the war cracks its knuckles not quite as before.

Reconnaissance

A dark foyer lets eyes adjust…a few minutes -
then move on: no breeze, quarter moon riding
cloud, romantics might think it beautiful: so to
auditorium, pure theatre now: centre stage the
set piece grave newly dug, its cross crowned by
helmet with fist-sized gash - cold truth repeats
itself: the strength of armour is not in the steel.

Traps

No abstract, the real thing...*hate:* synthesis of pervading
shite stink of what they smoked; the place is loaded too -
pictures askew... bog cistern primed: old hat, but here's
a new wheeze: behind door cat sound multi registered to
tease imagination: check the criticals... eye contact only,
but zero, *alles ist in ordnung* but here be dragons for sure.
We back off, leave note for the sappers, hating ourselves.

Bring On the Clowns

…. the old six hundred waiting on Cardigan,
army's poised, SSM's glory now, Go!Go!Go!
Wait! Lead driver Obie Walker's gone awol,
a waiting army stymied before starting: SSM
has can and full Monty fears: but no sky-fall!
Here idles no-hurry Obie from privacy doing
up fly: a cartoon dawn - we start-lined happy.

(*SSM – Squadron Sergeant Major*)

Off The Blocks

I'm all Aztec…no-sun still sends shivers;
sun stained boyhood, a fistful of summer
before *real* cuts in; thereafter adolescent
traumas, limbo, then a deja vu *Overlord*:
eventually rest before Rhine X: shirt off,
taking the rays with bottles of bad wine;
if I need a quiet worship, I sit in the sun.

(Overlord – code name for Normandy campaign 1944)

A Church Too Far

A left-to-die, shattered by shellfree… this community's
lapsed act of faith caught up and dead on its feet; inside
a litany of silence, imagined resonance of a bell dumped
from tower, defiant heater stamped with patents; debris
knee deep where a gasp of colour reveals Madonna with
half a child, she with fragile beauty, sad as if all love she
offered wasn't enough: I set her where sun might warm.

Sniper

A plot to raise the neck's short hairs -
with just one to play the starring role,
lighting almost perfect; second player
up stage acts cat-in-waiting, assuming
the Heckler's tactile symmetries to be
beautiful... no narrative needed: *now*
is Godot play...until the last full stop.

(Heckler: German sniper rifle)

A V1 Falls Silent 1945

Now you hear it - *that's good, it's going somewhere else,*
but now you don't - that Maserati crackle cuts out...go
formulaic: *height + speed = ?* which does *not* help - you
know neither: think *probability* - no... go for *possibility,*
it's less definite; you've had ten seconds since Maserati
conked...a load of *Bang* should've hit the deck by now:
where? when?...emphasis on the former – a total focus.

Saxony Nay 1945

War To War Summer

When the wind's easterly comes the scent
of Dresden...we patrol an edge of another
war - an Elbe's width divides us...it's low
profile between cupola flaps - silly to stop
one now in high summer heat; river's full
of what it carries; showing the flag a daily
routine hoping a west wind stays westerly.

The Not Forgotten

Replays like a grainy film: a near-post-war
patrol - 30 tons, bells, whistles, guns; ahead
Rosinante pulling cart, straw hat man busy
with whip: traffic closes...scared shitless by
us and everything, Rosinante takes off over
embankment, churns sailing a milky wash -
it's *keep going,* and Rosinante's still falling.

Cross Country

Stunned fields wasted - rough as an old dog's pelt,
a sensed dissonance builds to a threat, making my
Luger congruous in alert country swept by chilled
east wind in its breath; the tenuous circuit goes on
past places with blank watching windows - I stride
out like the beach boy I was in a dusk before dark:
limbo...how many measures required in a lifetime?

Handing Over

It's no-sweat transporters today - we move out,
deserting ennui, mosquitoes, things in the Elbe.
Reputation rides in before Russians, the village
we leave distraught - politics rule, not those left
to sweat. Easy riding we see Russian dust rising
as mirage morphing to flagged staff car, trucks,
hostile stares, *win one get one free* someone says.

The Fire Next Time

Its gene roots... flowers pure incendiary at
dragon's speed... *fire you're free!* Unleash
savage winds to super heat this generating
storm force of yourself - soon your captive
brothers will scent new rumours and rage;
go for wilderness, thicket and thorn: track
down spent forest, breathe new kingdoms.

Harz Mountains - 1945

The Other Place

This is the other place - a war coin's obverse:
forest rooted in centuries of itself…cleared to
fine tillage, villages, a schloss on improbable
crag, a serious beauty somehow diverting the
tides of conflict visiting like seasons; reality is
the shoulder plough stand-off forcing new life
into the old - creation in the essence of silence.

Farm Family – Harz 1945

Diversion is seldom total: a riptide took the men,
women closed ranks, life went on in the old cycle
limping a little - Grandpa minding geese, smoked
leaf cigarettes under a tree, Granny did children,
soup, the women everything else led by the sun…
slept warm with their cattle stabled below, a half
life of living…*Kursk* hanging like fog in the trees.

GOTTINGEN 1945 - Meditations

1.
Arrival

Man-cub out of jungle... I'd kiss the devil's arse
for that again: a city somehow fireproof – I from
the ash of everywhere swallowed it whole, not its
stone by stone reality - more the roots and effort
of ancient scholarship extolling an age of focused
attention on new creative symmetries concurring
with the hopes of beauty being a conduit to truth.

2.
The Beautiful Dead

That being my first sighting - a threshold
of new worlds beyond the mirage. On the
backs of the beautiful dead, a progress of
scholars in glory tread a fine line between
hope and belief in held-breath times after
war, reinforcements thrown in to take on
again the ever elusive abstraction of God.

3.
Snakes & Ladders

Too much baggage to absorb the affirmation
of something *other*, a firewall intelligence set
on facts of existence extending to boundaries
challenging thought - the snakes and ladders
endeavour of the simple soul frazzled almost
to ashes is remaindered with instinct enough
to sense fresh beginnings… is travelling still.

4.
Getting There

First step is the beginning of everything, terrain
reduces mirage, a slow unlocking - jungle world
turns to theatre where player, plot, denouement
hang on the edge of everything, straws in the fist
of opportunity if there's light enough to show its
there - morr instinct, sensed, not yet understood.
If there's point to progress, it's the getting there.

Nord Express – 1945

That step up from platforms gets me going… mahogany
panelling with gold squiggles, that old thirties' je ne sais
pas ce que exotic smell…I'm early with window seat, its
Calais - Kobnhavn all the way with a touch of history in
between. Steward asks if I require coffee, of course I do,
black no sugar, I'll keep things like this. What was *Club
Route* replays at a mile a minute… faster than last time.

(Club Route - British 2nd Army's axis of attack 1944-5)

Off The Lead

Strasbourg 5 a.m, the air metallic cool, a locomotive sighs, strains its way into yet another night handover time, dawn makes it sweet; never felt so free, could get off now and go walkabout everywhere, DP on the way to what comes next. *The Moment* now it's serious, the practical irrelevant: first chance. Stationmaster with lantern passes, he's the boss - I the product forever passing through. This *is* the moment...

(DP – Displaced person)

On The Loose

Singular moment - tail light of my train disappearing
into dawn: early Strasbourg like early anywhere else;
foot-recce turns up an oasis café fogged with Gitanes,
Gauloises…she behind counter has *the spark*, her hair
raven, *don't stare* she says, *only at beauty* my lips reply
lines like that so early say you're dangerous she flatters
back, *you'll want breakfast*? *That's fine for now* I say.

(*the spark*…that rarest gift…)

FRENCH CONNECTIONS

Avant Liberation - 1944

Dawn now - the square as night left it, tang of Seine,
pigeon checking out breakfast; a figure in doorway,
his army left at 0200 - *Last Tango in Paris* stuff, but
he wouldn't know…starts for Berlin, anywhere, has
to catch up: walks out: a *Maquis* gunsight following:
ritual now - place exact where guillotine once stood:
hate, fate, river mist: a shot… a puppet is unstrung.

Piaf's Paris 1945

A tricky year...bloody to beautiful one might say
and a crazy renaissance would do just fine; army
leave said *Paris* - lamb to the slaughter: a look at
the naughties, new tasty poisons, rain - so theatre
called, a last expensive seat: *who's Piaf? Ecoute!*
Then she's there, so small a focus, but that voice,
nuance, power...*Non je regrette rien*. Nor did we.

Last Lap 1947

Leave Pevensey...out onto marsh road, the best part,
slow down... enjoy: over right marsh cattle idle hock
deep in dyke mist round their half tree to scratch on;
where Weald rises a corn field's slashed with poppies
like a wound - I'm home; in leather helmet, goggles, I
feel a manqué Biggles, turn off at the *Lamb* for Hooe,
job, midday pint...mirage years slipping off my back.

HOPE COVE

Making Base

Fine shingle is best…lie in the scoop, wriggle body shape
deeper; I do one for Ma then pitch our tent. Full moon is
rising over the cliff and its wicked path that offers us the
deserted beach. We eat, warm out courtesy of driftwood
fire, hit our sacks; 2a.m, the sea's a flat calm with echoes
of gulls offshore: I skinny dip a moon path out to check -
turn, see all I've left behind, fight tide-pull back to beach.

Reef Building

I fly a shadow over the sharps and flats of a rock fall long
overtaken by sea; clamped in pincer jaws something jars:
I recognise a shadowed fuselage sea-encrusted - its tail fin
erect, defiant; Yankee, Brit, Hun – all expendable as their
ammunition: I wonder if they knew that - some never did.
I fly back over sea's gentle industry in reclamation mode;
in twenty years, job done: crustacean paradise - new reef.

Aberration

Driftwood flames the signal…the dip of phosphorescent oar blade, two men beaching dinghy; I pick a brandy keg, dead weight on my shoulder; companions loaded, I lead to cliff path, sheer-drop close; no coastguard, no trouble…the maid opens cottage door wide-eyed *face the wall my lovely while the gentlemen pass by* I say. Cellar safe, I pay in gold so they'll return; then to beach and waiting tide. Back to *now* I stoke up fire thinking brandy kegs: *come to bed* calls Mary.

ON THE EDGE

Fire Burn... Cauldron Bubble

Teifi estuary plus sentry hills - mid-March and late;
wordless, Ma turns towards the cliff path... I pause,
continue to beach: tide's halfway, leaving emptiness.
I fall back to beach-comb mode, driftwood. Needing
focus I collect, build, ignite craving salt wood's fired
intensities - brash, beautiful brief protection against
dark outriders moving in: I gather nurture and wait.

Sun and Shadow

Court yard at high noon ennui... shadow repeated cypress
gives teeth to a track indolent without cart-weighted wheel.
I try to write you something memorable...sleepy on elbows
but focus now...this Tuscan viper close - too close, its chain
mail coiled iridescent in sun warmed dust, a hair triggered
trap, primed...here's subject to make memorable! I pause
to reconsider what else I've missed in the summer's debris.

Painting

To paint I fix the chair and easel: sun is fiercely hot:
we've covered-up, Ma wearing floppy hat for shade.
I leave her intent... air full of the everywhere yellow
scented broom in a Roman silence not quite desolate
though clouds might make it so; I conjure hot colour
schemes in a drift of time - aqueduct short shadowed
endures, a hard edge of *now*, the contrast conclusive.

The End Game

Red-eyed, sky hurls its bolts...explosive but
not yet ready to explode, flash card trickery
devilling dumped possessions, this armchair
on three legs and hardback *Vasari;* all night
we do not speak, thought gelled around that
spark between us; game over, except to play
out each nuance of script to its denouement.

On the Last Day

Ma wakes me early *we must go home*...we pack, load
the cinquecento, drive to Pisa: even now she needs to
check Pisa's Tower far out in crazy tilt: *it's so Italian*
she says, *wish I had their style...* We fly home Alitalia;
her painting yesterday wasn't what I'd seen - neither
aqueduct nor broom on site - mementoes left behind;
she dozes somehow remote, deep down...journeying.

On The First Day

So you are gone - that rare theme and look closed like a book
as they attend you there settling your body, tidying your hair,
fact blurs my eye, sun behind a cloud, a milk float passing by,
a reality off axis - seemingly obscene as if you had never been;
nothing matters without hope, even to the tremor on my rope
as one remaining belay shifting, fails... a falling climber spins
in the rush and *now* of fleeting images: what is to come begins.

Wolf Dawn

At midnight of a dream the first of grey ...
the very first, in multi shades of silence, of
dew printed pad in forever forest, nothing
disturbed in the night's stealthy narrative;
grey flows separately now; a spit off shore
lake freezing round them, silhouetted bear
with cub. Lighter now grey settles to wait.

Beach Game

Emphatic place, a mood of emptiness, sea sluiced off the east horizon, reaction is to walk as conversation lags: he'd say *you're beautiful,* but the wind's too full of icy rivets for artless observation and logic of the outer senses scores: so they search for shells - ones you hear the sea in and so reason damps the silly heats of passion... how the state of truth surprises! Groups of seabirds back from land stab at their reflections while running tides of demons swirl gritty sea, making people islands.

Presque Vu

So nearly I had the drop on you, seizing at inklings, those
loaded hints of some enormous future: came that sense of
breaking through... the flashback imaging spun at speeds
of memory- kingdoms lit in full zap and lilt of colouration
entireties divorced from wit in *almost* recognition, neither
the artist's epiphany nor dream - cogencies to peripherals
dissolving the very thought like candles overcome by dark.

Impressionist

Past first light - brush strokes on a canvas, colours of a sprung artery, images hang in minds like bats; sun shots slick as foxes cross open country flattering with warmth, each etched second strikes its attitude - at home on gallery walls. Artistry ghosts in negatives of wash: imagination takes fix: scented draw of wood smoke, mirage men, vehicles - then stops short: old Chanticleer breaks out from dream, crazing a masterpiece of earth and sky.

Gentillesse de Coeur...

The Lady Imogen virginal drawbridge secured, had this
forenoon of a sultry day fixed her favours to the lance of
Sir Glamour - unhorsed at first joust...such the vagaries
of perfect womanhood displeased and so fatigued by the
inanities of the Royal Entourage, who is bloody minded
(favour has an obverse) but she knows the score: at first
light sleepless Sir G seeks dragons to fire-up expectation.

The Very Idea

Spun like the spider yo-yoing on its silk...gossamer
as thought, the have, have not of *nearly* accepted as
a wavelength seeking focus in attic darks of a mind
not perfectly tuned to all subtleties of inspiration at
speeds somewhere between dream and recognition:
no formula for this, instinct may be better than gun
sight focus to bring close enough for words to touch.

The Beam

A good luck acorn missed by the pigs, he gnarls and girths to
a mighty oak awaiting broadsides, ships of the line while fops
fopped and George grew even madder...until Trafalgared by
loggers and their farting horses - such dreams: alas, his short
straw destiny's far away in the sticks; vertical again he holds
up everything, too tough for woodworm, complexion good as
Auden's - brooding by the G&Ts he dreams a new Napoleon.

Cymru Am Byth

Putting Down Roots

Cutting engine I slip into river sounds… movement, cadences
in registers of forever; now deep in the peaty waters, shadows
melt into under-tree darks… *now you're awake guys, I've a fly
tied especially for you…* I take it in: silence riding river voices,
sheep path over scree, silver birch by Twm's cave. All as ever.
I make base on soil inches over rock - tent pegs hard to locate,
I battle the last while kettle sings…there's time for everything.

(*Twn Sion Catti – Welsh answer to Robin Hood*)

Late Comer

A caul of sky drawstrung to earth's foundations, two fields away
the last tv light extinguishes - the final braying politician poured
into limousine and removed to vanished hills; this window sticks
(rain rains, wood warps) fighting, yields on a pitch of nipped pig
and in slips silence as a tired man to his fireside full of the world,
dumb with it… even to the river I know is there working its stars
like rosaries; inside tattered, cold, he brings nothing - everything.

On The Way to Pontafynach

It's early, air fizzy as champagne... a mountain taste that's
never lost. I trace a graph's sharps, flats and fix... the pony
wrought white against sky, myth from imagination's far off
kingdom, luck's fairest chance, all sky cloudless: *take a look*
I say, *I don't do magic often.* Gill's coffee pauses half way...
it's mountain-still, sun rising: *perfection or just close...* I ask
myself. She's smiling *how often? Once a lifetime* I say, *enjoy.*

(Pontarfynach – Devil's Bridge)

Sign Posts

Three with fingers to make sure…if foreign you'll be
no wiser… try *Cwmddyldaibach, Ysbytystwyth?* Quite.
However, Ysbytystwyth is classed as an inspirational
honey pot asking *Illiterati* to joust with original ideas.
Finger post for my path west shows *Tipperary or Bust*
painted red. Refreshing that, artistic joker with time
out and humour to spare, leavening the national loaf.

Sleeping Out

Around midnight a breeze creeps in from Atlantis
tuning in wires pole high on their paths elsewhere,
their strung notes at the far away edge of a destiny
already found; there's skyline with far star chatter
in magic registers - mood changing at light's pace:
Atlantis raises its game, strikes up to fix a moment
of subtle cadence into a night's haunting discourse.

Before Llyn Brianne

When it's this steep lean back...give the old girl a slack rein;
flooding has begun an inch deep - foundation for those black
fathoms to come. There's a house its gable aslant, a couple of
bans: people's lives, times past, a depth of stillness perversely
carrying its own energy igniting again what lifetimes become:
cattle grazing, echo of fallen pail, cadences, a *frisson* of voices,
lives living out years as long ago bells holding their resonance.

(*Llyn Brianne – a flooded valley in mid-Wales*)

Almost There

Watching dawn come up, suggestion only; Craig's scree slips
still messing with gravity... I can hear its rattle and slither as
it settles into another day's redemption. Now the sun returns
with summer; testing the Pysgottwr's chill, I swim to the pool,
dive through green turning black where origins hold me back:
hunter hunted - flirting with a dark that offers no suggestions,
till my breath runs out fine-testing all I am, edging the eternal.

(Craig - a high point adjacent to Twm Shon Catti's cave)

Accentuating a Negative

The time's pretty near perfect, a fly-life surface active with raindrop impressions - not that many; I settle... take stock, there is a completeness here - ancient rhythms that become the changing and the changeless tuned to follow the eternal patterns of what seems absolute – for me, the atavistic need to compact eternity into what is perceived as actual without strings. My cast drifts past - no takers: no problems either.

Hiraeth

Maybe fighting a tedious present… action does
the business - takes to the road travelled before
in darkness where bat's radar reigns. Arriving,
engine & wipers cut: in flow bells of confluence
ringing down its waters; now it's *feel… senses*:
iron bridge a shudder of river passion - scented
air a coverlet for skylines and all I know is here.

(*Hiraeth* – a longing for one's home country)

In The Cage

Escarpment levels out… a Dutch cheese moon rough-rides
the sky line. Singular in confusions of rock something odd,
box-like, becomes trap knocked up from strut and chicken
wire; I check it out - there's a mountain crow inside, raggy
and wet, been here for days…if you are crow from egg you
do crow things, upset farmers who set clever traps…a war,
two actually, each in pursuit of survival: tonight's dilemma.

First Curlew

A negative drift to the dark days
that last for ever...Atlantic cloud
its theatrical glower a more-than
take on any time darks, its mood
sized hair shirt; now switch off...
switch on to this longed-for tune,
fine glass fragile in a warm wind.

French Quarter New Orleans

Love Affair

Jazz rides out, trad mostly - unreasonably, I'm listening
out for West Coast; Mississippi does foundation, Jazz is
the roof over everything. It's *Mardi Gras* - delta clammy
hot; a marriage procession swings along to the sober bit
and the Quarter dances: I grab Gill…she's feather light,
close - I'm dizzy with love. At O'Brien's we laze outside,
drink icy Buds, look at each other catching the moment.

Honeymoon River

Twain once spoke of Mississippi shifting sands, extant maybe inhibiting night-freighting...but never reining-in that age old continental voyage of itself. Now a night spell hugs round us, moon's getting full, staging's set (making all the detail right): we know we see this world's top side only, but now it's all we want: Armstrong's *wonderful world* is chiming and we dance to the surge and spray of our paddle boat's tune.That's close.

Atlantic Dawn

Vacuum - a passage of particles, atoms at high speed,
dark the absolute; infinity shifts an elbow - transition
the merest concept *not dark,* a grey hair-thin splitting
of space as all colour reinvents itself in the impending
absence of dark, a break from what had been eternal;
somewhere its parameters…a slow-burn first light on
its measured schedule to an ending: the one certainty.

Anza Borrego

Desert Flowering

Scrub, snakes, silence - Ocotillo scarlet catches the eye:
San Andreas upheaval too, areas of serious indigestion.
A gentler world in springtime after rain: with laser eye,
high boots (rattlers not all asleep), we go sub scrub to a
garner of shy *Milk Maid*, the symmetry of *Thorn Apple,*
bridal white, fragile against a harsh regime, a gossamer
supercharger forever challenging the absolute of desert.

Going Solo

All arena exploding…stung furies of colour,
Apache, Sioux, Cheyenne - a fired levitation
hunting the plains where buffalo turn dawn
to dusk: alas, all that a one man enactment:
frenzy dies – a horizon fades to reservation;
audience applauds his authenticity - grease
paint, ribboned tomahawk, its plastic blade.

Any Time Anywhere...

At Annabelle's

**Buck's Fizz... fuelling rearguard's
remnant passion locked inside the
encirclement cutting supplies that
so far never failed; the last couple
centre stage cuts mustard in silky
unison... blonde in close support;
Buck's Fizz... who needs oxygen?**

Scent and Sensibility

Rye… Cinq Port without sea, a magic hall
of forest stillness before the felling of trees
crafted, loved to this oil haunting presence
they became; high up the measured arc of
pendulum controls its clock's reply - sweet
talking to reconnect me to a half imagined
place where lifetimes ago, sentience began.

The Smell of Green Apples

Crossing last infinities of sleep…. in orbit again
in the ring of dawn chorus playing the acoustics
of an empty street; tactile the rough of blankets,
sensuous encounter…then the everywhere scent
of *Granny Smith* - intense, petticoat tart, oxygen
of the dawn's first breath pulling you back on to
the honed edge of sentience - it's inside you now.

Settling the First Born

At first two of you - then that time of owl alert
for moonshot - so three await sleep and hunger
hour: but your first born fed, is restless - a new
beginning impacts itself too soon perhaps; now
owl in shadow-silent hunger quarters... stoops.
Moon set and first light attend as a newly risen
star thumb in place, takes fragile hold on sleep.

A Time of Year

The two of them baby at breast, an iphone playing
something Lennon; beyond bedded council colours
brash, beautiful, old men benched along the tennis
courts wipe their eyes - peer on swivelled necks for
ball, for shot or anything, always seconds too latte;
outside the troubled stare of history, mother, child,
in the pose which warms cathedrals…Pietá update.

On The River Wear - Durham

The water black as Guinness - maybe not quite;
the plan: to Prebends Bridge and back; a strafe
of summer squall pits river face into mock rises.
I watch you deep in reverie - Egypt's kingdoms,
Isis and dreams moving old worlds on to today;
we look at each other, smile: you're back! I row
whirlpools, wake - sun steaming shirts as we fly.

Old Souls

Gravitas of adzed bean to pulpit, still that sense
he had blessed and named this blip on infinity's
screen before yet somehow failed: now a sprung
trap chance of a much or little destiny resetting,
waits; cradling now in fear of letting her slip, he
gives love this time, sees her search for anything
of him till starburst eye-to-eye...and congruence.

Run Fox - 1955

A shadowed end-game... this fuselage - a beached fish
overgrown, a glimpsed insignia and history's revealed:
replay stage entrance: no fuel no fire, silence regroups
except for the tick-tick of metal cooling under rainbow
slicks of oil; canopy's closed: fox to earth when hounds
run wild; time winds down... forest rewrites itself with
sentinel forces with a song to sing in the onshore winds.

Cave Horses

Those struck moments...still the everything
of what they were - caught by creative gene,
human eye, to play back split seconds stilled
in a first imagining beyond the ape, to make
colour, find rock face canvas in time beyond
need of food, shelter, to repeat those sprung
energies of enactment...fear and flying hoof.

Rock Art

Arcadia's obverse - slate scree to razor the boot
where damp greys rule Ok, even to leaf, branch
of the dumb acorn-to-oak freaking from crevice
and crack. But brilliant on slate canvas: flowers
that grow nowhere but in the heart - creation of
free spirits in mockery of murky grey. Long live
imagination's anarchy - its mintings, its coinage.

Cretan Shepherd

Imagine him first... sheep close, something
symbiotic, extant since first legend, juniper
and rock; a simple narrative - survival in a
given that has to be found - time at its pace
of dawns to dusk, Agamemnon to air drop;
when the sun sets shepherd, flock are gone
where new days become; It is written... Is.

Air Port Guard – Heraklion

First to last he's Cretan, if there's in between
it's cloaked in high summer day to night with
neither dusk nor dawn as the season yields its
harvest: to him the symmetries of life are lost
in cattle tides of *somewhere else: getting there,*
an affront tensing stance and touch of trigger
finger on first pressure... half way to the next.

Field Craft for Beginners

Come gently to your time of taking - like autumn,
when you *feel* do it deeply - *be* your camouflaging
tree, sap to stillness; make the most of shadowing
but be circumspect, it's hard to predict; note how
live things yield, elusive lines that flow, still - then
move again. All stage is yours: hit the boards *now*
fast and away as if life depended… it does – today.

Tank Range at Tyneham

Killers' country, fields torn as old blankets tacked together
with barbed wire; such woods that remain stand splintered,
emptied of everything; there are no straight lines here, only
contour, the hump of a barrow and the jangled angularities
of tanks shot up for targets. Genesis is in returning seasons,
death the erosion of barrow, turret, under ancient skylines:
sunset… a windhover rides high, content to live and let die.

Enjoy Your Meal

With the first course I serve a Chateau Neuf: Jack spins out a
story and is back to overpopulation; Jill rests her little bosom
on the cloth, talks us through an oven setup she's changing to
while candles burn out time weeping tears of wax. After puds
and cheese I contemplate a saw-edged plonk, hesitate…seems
a mean restraint, so re-fill waiter-like with more top end stuff
to that just-so mark - watching conscience fill each emptiness.

Clearing Up

Fusty shelves crammed with Common Law & Tort
shack-up together - a fly does its feet on an iphone.
Blah sys their solicitor earning a hundred guineas:
they understand him perfectly...two accomplished
enemies across the table once rooted oak: they sign
a settled peace, the fly departs; he sees her without
his ring: life so far unthought draws up beside him.

Boys in Blackberry Woods

The sun hangs his hawk on a string, burning autumn rich
a kingdom... the trees sing: hand to mouth they're struck
sensing deeper rides of appetite. Pied as piper insurgency
flights blood, brain - they loiter edgily as if unearthed by
forest gods who grow each his cleft foot, horns - manhood
in vessels too small; relenting, gods silence siren trees, put
spell on *hold*... a dream to keep close by, one day re-enter.

Chorale

Finale's voices resonating…wave on wave
in point, counter point from pyx to pulpit;
time to absorb a pillar's elegance - a lift of
voices in stained glass moted space: I slide
from rationality sensing otherness close in,
sun through the drift of mirage - a pulsing
as of butterfly unhusked flighting into air.

Eiger – North Face

Nearest pitch to random fates, chance, god et al,
multidimensional living force because it's there,
life itself: feel….imagine a near certain one-way
challenge which passes reason all the way to the
struck-match flare of necessity - a singular very
human imperative which sailed medieval minds
in *chance it* mood to the far shores of possibility.

Bag Lady

Rosie lit out from a mean inheritance and kept going:
travelled, tried everything... even a sappy state called
love...flying too close to the sun she melted her wings;
she headed west where all the gold is, filling her crazy
pram with treasures: ocotillo flowers, things beautiful
not letting go. Rosie is out west now feeding sea birds:
ocean chills out after a thousand miles, likewise Rosie.

Conversions

Stables in apotheosis - it's a new chapel now:
how easily horse and harness slip away, then
a new imprint becomes; but it's this magical
scent of snuffed candles that hooks and reels
you in as if a door has just been opened on a
holding pattern - old horses, new piety - this
the place to re-start journeying, and you do.

Sammy's Search

In scant shade Sammy watches this mile-long freighter
crossing on heat-jazzy tracks, intrusive world in desert
silence deep as eternity itself: furnace heat replays new
devildom, gods fight for hegemony over what's old hat
to Sammy who seeks meaning where it lies...his driven
search for what he has to find not realised yet, fired by
the old drill: always coming closer by not standing still.

Redundancies

Her first shy kiss of love, that *Zing*
its recognition before the badlands
leave train goes; I remember them,
how they became - the leave trains
not returning: new cast, old script:
dulce et decorun est pro patria mori *
timeless patron of the dispossessed.

(*it is sweet and proper to diefor the fatherland*) *

Girl in a Treetop

She climbs tree easy and animal into other-world green,
stands top cat sprung against sky: tree spins rumours in
the wind; *I am* she thinks – but behind safe night light is
I am not as space falls thinly...she clings white-knuckled
in an ache of vertigo before instinct intercedes, confirms
with *I am...I am* - and a lesson is learned. Released from
babyhood she descends, one day to tell it to her children.

Florentines

Piazza Della Signora: where the established kind
of dogma did for Savonarola by fire: such echoes
never die, the open window tells me so. No moon
with the ash of darkness falling like a mood over
riding even *ennui,* with you brooding a thousand
miles away - shark fins cutting ocean in between;
bed: *lost my bloody toothbrush! Use mine* you say.

Double Entendre:
From a painting by Wyeth

**The picture seems not to seek regeneration:
fought-through forest, long firebreak centre
staging an upturned helmet refilled with old
cones; feeble sunlight, scatterings of needles
fallen to early frosts detail a framed stillness
of history rewinding lost ambition... but old
cones source new props for a next just cause.**

It Was As If

There's sprung presence on this touch
point of Down electrifying the air like a
rung bell's aftersong - a gravitas poised
as if to crack the ineffable offering a ley
lined trapeze timed seizure first footing
that lit city with walls imagination high,
ready to fall to a one illuminated insight.

Wintering Out

Windbreak pines with hippo hides, a trad caravan in fairground colours, a piebald rugged when Jack Frost pretties her ears, and Alsatian on its running lead; every dawn a rasp of stone on axe blade, drift of woodsmoke: travellers on the edge of everything haunting distances in their blood. Spring...camp is deserted, a footprint in the ash of an all-winter fire.

A Rose From Summer

Summer tired as an old dog, a castle rising
course by course, chip and ring of mason's
chisel biting stone until teeth of battlement
imposes a new skyline, symbol of conquest
already won; in a final cavity this dog rose
cut with love, something to be entrusted to
legend: all that is encompassed in a flower.

Karpaz & Co

Monastics and Karpaz cats…those close to heaven,
those far from food: dress code bible black…habits
in particular, plus felines in their shapes of famine:
a dichotomy of interest here: Thomas Aquinas and
angels on a pin - gravitas rising as steam to the sun
while multitudes stave off eternity; the sea looks on
blank and blue: *feed them* I cry in fury, *two will do*!

(Karpaz – the pointy part of Turkish Cyprus)

Under the Algarroba Tree

Karpaz… a late dissonance of Turkish jazz with
rutting donkeys chiming incidental congruencies
testing the long taut thread of evening when *lack*
by far exceeds the sum of everything; he rewinds
a yesterday: she's close - steals an olive, decorous
with stone (he spits his): will she one day be real?
He fills, refills: another carob falls - and the next.

Vikings

From the silt of old rivers academe found us.
shards of broadsword, the grain of forests in
the timber of ships which sailed carrying the
bite of conquest and survival... the scholars'
fix, icons living on in all dimensions...blood,
genes of heritage; out of silt emerges legend,
actuality wearing T-shirts like the rest of us.

Dream of a Golden Flower

A radiance Van Gough almost found, upstaging everything except the focus of itself plus awe, its dream lit brilliance all in *my* dream! Could alter ego be teasing? So what...I'll make lovely, green finger everywhere, dig prettily with the robin on my spade - while conversing to keep wakefulness at bay: here be psycho dream powered by cliché.

O'Brien's Army

Is consolidating…wall to lamp stand, approved
by canines also staking territory - sophisticated
multi sited space for all O'Brien's cyclopic eyes
seeing everything: you look up - instinct maybe,
it blinks… X rates *just for reference* as O'Brien
deploys forces slow and sure as hemlock - while
dogs stay happy a future becomes: 1984? Close.

Time Warp

Urban early... first train on circle line: Agincourt
is now: close by with pipe teasing the melody of a
long ago song, he of small stature, shoulder tuned
to drawn bow, lank hair greasy where bowstrings
sleep under cap with the lice. Empowered behind
his driven stake he plays a waiting game, bow tall
as he: in such a dawn find him once - never again.

Easter Service

For as long as it takes they wait...women in mantillas, girls
in white; then the priest's intonation cloistering the echoes:
a great arena fills with alchemies of sun-shafts shifting tints
of scarlet-to-carmine; aisle-bent for consecration they move
serenely in atmospheric distance; for those of us from other
worlds a sense of loss...colours dwindle, a camera whispers
straining to seize what remains of this rainbow's other side.

Poppy

In multitudes - Flanders to a slash of
cornfield scarlet and each November
buttonhole the *in memoriam* - a reset
consciousness instilled; but Poppy as
singular, this conscience… its flaring
petal delicate as skin, an eye that has
seen everything - symbol of life itself.

Drift

In the tides' rinse and polish a coast is drawn to Dungeness,
shingle beach in world populations rests, moves in perpetual
pilgrimage towards the pull of something sensed; sometimes
perhaps in boredom, history intervenes – sea skims a soul or
two forwards or back a thousand dawns, as inconsequential
as the breaking wave. It may be that all begins at Dungeness
with purgatories of souls seeking salvation and keeping faith.

Notes on the Hunter

A tiger circles in his head, that rolling gait of day
on day, with thirsty herded clichés on goat paths
to the pub, mock gothic poxed by stucco: this old
thicket sits hunter, hunted clotted round another
empty glass; when water hole dries he'll die - not
of thirst alone...but from having that far mirage
dissolve from the horizons - never coming closer.

Breakers: a view of car wrecks

The pile…skyline of itself plus two fingers at
gravitational laws; a jazzy tarnish of chrome
hung over one time zippy waxed skyblue and
flourish of pink - a child's eye take on the cut
and bluster of middling shunt and a head-on;
closer there'll be rust, tang perhaps of blood:
a sensing of what there is still to comprehend.

Countdown

At times of imagination, a church spire in silhouette
suggests a rocket's prosthetic line with a gantry web
of scaffolding round crumbling stone poised as if for
blast-off crammed with its all souls' computer crews
with Mars as staging post for that portal to destinies
glimpsed but never held: the seeker's honeyed pitch
to track and hold the narrative of greater sentience.

Mind Slip

A fidget of tectonic plates jacks up the desert,
a village morphs to spoil as sky clouds over -
time tweaks a destiny or two: this wife dream
warped in dizzy light stolen from recollection
wicked as echo stares face-on at an image she
can't remember, old worlds with roots to find
as time weaves its tapestry resets the moment.

Storm Bells

Richter scale fury shudders tower - bells poised
against stays await *look to…* pulling off in tight
succession to make the round then repeat, their
flight an echo of history - ultimate facedown of
what is elemental, a confident flexing of muscle
in the magic of music, stave-loaded lyrics flying
with wings of storm birds highriding the winds.

Connection

Thos Eyre fecit 1662... engraved on my
bell, a relationship here: Tom the man
passing on high tech skills of centuries,
creating music from brute iron: I tease
him off stay - back to rest, a resonance,
something uttered in the fust of church
silence, a contact received - a presence.

Echo Chamber

Songs not the singers…they're still here blended
with the never changing *now* of centuries, a mew
of buzzard, two rivers chiming into one - they're
a given far from singers who once trod this path,
absences real as winds toying with sky-borrowed
pelt of the lake below…the solitary scenario as a
man struggles to fire up the conjectures of recall.

On The Chancel Arch

The Judgement of course - propaganda direct
for the Sunday pews gawking at rich gold leaf,
fine-ground ultramarine for the smugly saved,
red oxide for the rest; in from toil on the strips
they existed from dawn to plague - redemption
plucked from small hungers only, a fine season
and waking warm - maybe in bewildered hope.

Bloomsbury Church Berwick, Sussex

Over the fields from Alfriston, Sussex sun, Downs
on their way to Seaford Head; I, solitary audience
contemplate centuries' given beliefs versus *Lit Crit*
coterie assertions: Pound, Eliot, Woolf L&V... the
human condition *real,* an anti atavistic take on life
of here and now, intrusive elbows as sharp as ever
in a cleric's ribs - a local ecclesiastical conundrum.

Island in the Stream

Sensing all its yesterdays... follow instincts: find
runaway briar patch - earthquaked potting shed
with attitude; sun-up gets to centre stage around
midday, tree people hitch up shadows like skirts;
Dionysus and Pan stoned now, wake at midnight,
see Pepys bury his gold as Pudding Lane fires up.
Demeter in straw hat keeps it growing and green.

In The Geriatric Ward

This night is a crawl of hours: at some time between 3 a.m.
and medication, the laugh rises to a crescendo, not sharing
the joke; here Grendel is no legend... Daedalus, slung high
in sling, curses in his labyrinth of despair: soft admonitions
soothe: nurse's flashlight flits jack-o'-lantern between beds,
the popeyed demons slip back to shadow; so slowly now the
caress of first light, firing the look of yet another tomorrow.

Candle Power

The fust of history, its stones still settling-in
after a thousand years… a voltage bridging
centuries; in a place like this you can light a
candle for pennies, I do one for Prometheus
bless him, one for me in case…but fire them
all… they'd roast the arse of darkness, force
into light what hides, digs so deep into cover.

At Ninety Two

If like history I had to repeat, I'd opt Swiss:
avoid middle-classness, public schools and a
squint: I'd apply myself to maths and things
that wind-up, join as an apprentice in Basle,
realise clocks less fun but safer than clitoris,
and mind my business… if Hitler got round
to think of invasion, I'd join the Swiss Navy.

En Route to the Crem…

Pussy Cat – if you'd like a church stop-off
en passant, feel free: expensive though, an
extra solemn shoulder shunt, clergyman's
spiel; don't bother with bells - though you
might fancy a quick *Plain Hunt* just for us,
you ringing 4th, I on 2nd - swapping places
to carry the tune, a song we sang together.

How It Might Be

Nearly there…Sanatorium Hill, golf club's spiky yellow gorse traps; I'm in Marmite jar on back seat; close now Beachy Head and coast guard dwellings before they fell off the edge. A touch more towards Birling Gap…this'll do fine: sweet Downs misty mauve inland - Marmite cap removed, a sea breath fidgets barbequed me for take off. So…maybe I'm off to discover myself. Watch this space.

Acknowledgements

My special thanks to Kathy Robinson – without her dedicated work, incredible patience and humour when I was wall climbing in frustration at something that did not really matter much, this book would never have escaped the depths of my computer. It's our book Kathy…hooray for us!